DORLING KINDERSLEY READERS

BEGINNING
1
TO READ

First day at gymnastics

Written by Anita Ganeri

A Dorling Kindersley Book

Jenny tugged at the sleeves
of her new leotard.
Her mum tied her hair up.

leotard

Jenny was going to gymnastics
for the first time.
What would it be like?

Anya had been to
gymnastics before.
"The lesson is really fun!"
said Anya.

The teacher was Ms. Sims.
She turned on the warm-up music.
The children hopped, skipped and
jumped.

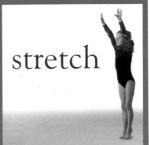

stretch

After that, they all stretched
their arms up in the air . . .

and then down to touch their toes.

"Spread out now and
find a big space on a mat,"
said Ms. Sims.
"Today Kate and Holly
will show you some moves.
We'll start with
a forward roll."

mat

Kate tucked in her head and
pushed with her feet.
She rolled over.
Jenny did it
on her very first try!

Next Kate did a backward roll.
Jenny did not find this so easy.
She couldn't roll over.

roll

"Put your hands by your ears,"
said Ms. Sims. "Now roll and push."

11

Kate then showed them
how to make different shapes
on the mat.
She lay on her back and
raised her arms and legs.

Then she lay on her tummy
to make an arch.

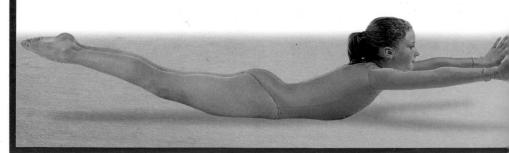

The class tried the shapes.
"Remember to stretch,"
said Ms. Sims.

Next Holly did a handstand.
She kicked her legs
up into the air.

Then Anya tried.
"Kick harder and
pull your legs together,"
said Ms. Sims.

Next Kate showed them
how to balance.
She lifted up one leg.

She stretched that leg
out to the side.
Then she stood
very still.

balance

The whole class
had a turn at balancing.
Jenny lifted one leg and
tried to keep very still.
But it was hard not to wobble!

"You almost did it," said Ms. Sims.
"Hold out your arms
to help you to balance."

The class split into groups next.
Anya and Jenny went
to the springboard
with their group.

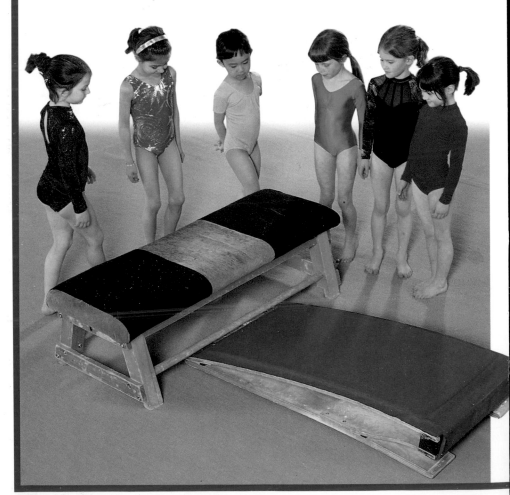

step

Holly showed them
how to step onto
the springboard and
jump off.

They went to the bars next.
Holly put both hands on the bar
and swung backwards and
forwards.
Then she let go and landed
on the soft foam.

Ms. Sims lifted Jenny up to the bar and helped her to swing.

bars

Holly climbed onto
the high beam.
She jumped up into the air and
bent her knees
as she landed perfectly.

beam

"You will be able to do that
when you are bigger,"
Ms. Sims told the class.
"First you must learn to balance
and walk on the floor beams."

Jenny walked carefully
along the floor beam.
She kept her back straight and
her arms stretched out.

Then she jumped off neatly.
"Very good, Jenny,"
said Ms. Sims.
"You have done well today."

The lesson was over.
"So soon?" Jenny asked sadly.
Ms. Sims put the music on.

The children walked
in time to the music and
lined up to say goodbye.

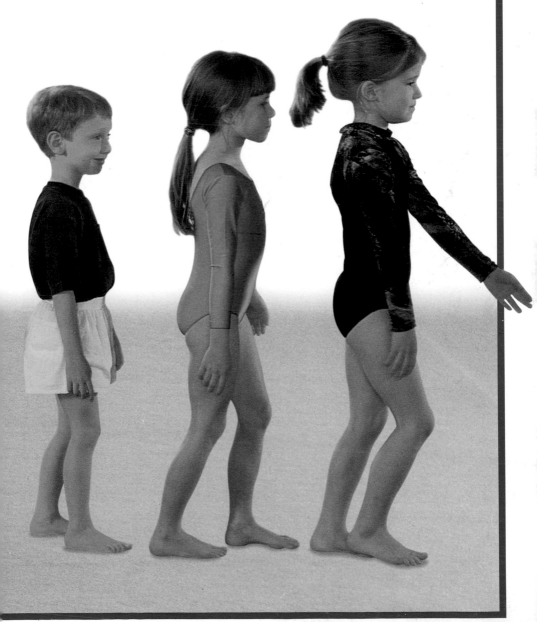

"Do you want to come again next week?" asked Jenny's mum. "Oh yes!" said Jenny.

One day I'll be a famous gymnast, thought Jenny.
I'll balance on one leg.
I'll swing on the bars.
I'll jump on the high beam.
And I won't wobble!

Picture word list

leotard

page 4

balance

page 17

stretch

page 7

step

page 21

mat

page 8

bars

page 23

roll

page 10

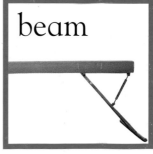
beam

page 24

32